fullpower™
safety comics

People Safety Skills for Teens and Adults

Irene van der Zande
Illustrated by Amanda Golert

relationsafe™
SKILLS FOR LIFELONG SAFETY AND SUCCESS

A publication of Kidpower Teenpower Fullpower International

Copyright And Permission To Use Information

Copyright Information

Fullpower Safety Comics: People Safety Skills for Teens and Adults. © 2015. All content in this book is copyrighted to author Irene van der Zande, Kidpower Teenpower Fullpower International founder and executive director. No part of this publication may be reproduced in any form or by any electronic or mechanical means, including information and retrieval systems, without prior written permission of the author or her designated representative.

Reproduction Information

Prior written permission must be obtained for reproducing any part of this publication in any form. However, a wealth of resources including some articles and handouts from this book are available for free on the Kidpower.org website. For information about how to obtain permission for different kinds of content use, please visit www.kidpower.org or contact the author at safety@kidpower.org.

Use of Content for Personal Learning or for Teaching Others

With proper acknowledgment, readers are encouraged to use knowledge from the Kidpower Teenpower Fullpower programs about self-protection, confidence-building, advocacy, personal safety, positive communication, child protection, leadership, team-building, and self-defense strategies and skills in their personal lives and professional activities.

We ask that readers tell people about Kidpower Teenpower Fullpower International when they use any examples, ideas, stories, language, and/or practices that they learned from our program, and let others know how to reach our organization.

Please note that permission to use content from our copyrighted programs verbally and in person is NOT permission to publish or duplicate any part of this content in any written or digital form in print or online, including in articles, lesson plans, research papers, videos, newsletters, books, videos, podcasts, websites, etc. These uses require separate permission as described above.

Restrictions

Unless people or agencies have an active agreement with Kidpower Teenpower Fullpower International, they are not authorized to represent themselves or give the appearance of representing themselves as working under our organization's auspices. This means that individuals and groups must have an active certification or agreement with our organization to be authorized to teach, promote, or organize workshops or other presentations using the Kidpower, Teenpower, Fullpower program names, workshop names, reputation, or credentials. Please visit www.kidpower.org or e-mail safety@kidpower.org about our instructor certification and center development programs.

Liability Disclaimer

Each situation is unique, and we can make no guarantee about the safety or effectiveness of the content or techniques described in this material. We do not accept liability for any negative consequences from use of this material.

Kidpower Teenpower Fullpower International
Office   *831-426-4407 or (USA) 1-800-467-6997*
E-mail   *safety@kidpower.org*
Web page   *www.kidpower.org*
Address   *P.O. Box 1212, Santa Cruz, CA 95061, USA*

Table Of Contents

Welcome To Fullpower!

Using your "full power" to stay safe with people

What is Fullpower?

Fullpower is our name for the adult programs of Kidpower Teenpower Fullpower International, a nonprofit organization dedicated to teaching people of all ages and abilities how to stay safe, act wisely, and believe in themselves.

What is People Safety?

"People Safety" means people being emotionally and physically safe with people, including themselves and others. Knowing and practicing People Safety strategies and skills can prepare you to have better relationships; advocate effectively for the well-being of yourself and others; become a powerful, respectful leader; and stay safe from most bullying, harassment, abuse, assault, and abduction.

How to use this book

Read the explanations and stories with the Fullpower Friends characters. Think about which strategies and skills you already know and use all the time-and which ones you need to learn or to remember to use. If an example is not relevant for you, think of how you can apply this idea to a situation you have faced or might face. And please let us know so we can share your example with others.

Make the Fullpower Put Safety First Commitment on page 6.

How to practice

Go over the Discussions and Practices on pages 71 to 77. Whether you are reading this book for yourself or to help others to learn, please remember:

- Learning and practicing People Safety is best done in a way that is fun and useful rather than scary or overwhelming. Focus on skills and ways to be as safe as possible rather than dwelling on all the bad things that might happen.

- People learn better by doing than by being told what to do. As much as you can, give yourself and those important to you chances to practice every skill shown in this book. Take the time to role-play the situations that happen in the stories. Think about and discuss what the Fullpower Friends characters say and do to keep themselves and others safe.

- Teach and learn by doing the skills in small steps when necessary, and look for progress rather than perfection. Learn and teach new skills step-by-step. We are all on our own paths in learning People Safety skills. Focus on growth rather than on trying to be perfect. Mistakes are part of learning. You don't have to be perfect to be great!

- Make using People Safety a part of your everyday life. The more you practice, the easier the skills are to remember and the more they become a natural part of the way you act in the world.

Share with others

Finally, you and the important people in your life will have fewer problems and more fun with each other if you all have clear agreements about what you expect and how you will handle conflict. Share these ideas and skills with you your family, friends, colleagues, co-workers, and others. Use People Safety everywhere you go—at home, at school, in your neighborhood, on public transportation, at work, while shopping, on trips, and while doing recreational activities.

Introducing The Fullpower Friends

Come join the Fullpower Friends—Mike, Rosa, Mei Lin, and Talib—while they show how to use their "full power" to stay safe and have better relationships with people.

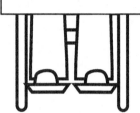

Mike loves everyone and has a great sense of humor. He worries about whether people will like him.

This book has examples, stories, and practices of "People Safety" skills and ideas. People Safety means making safe choices and protecting your feelings when others act thoughtless, mean, scary, or dangerous.

People Safety also means knowing how to stay in charge of what you say and do so that you are always acting safely and respectfully towards others, even when you feel upset.

Using People Safety skills will help you to have more fun, develop positive relationships, feel more confident, and stay safe from most bullying, abuse, and other violence.

Mei Lin is proud of who she is and a strong advocate. Her difficulty in compromising can cause conflicts.

Talib is caring and trustworthy. His shyness about speaking up can cause others to misunderstand or ignore him.

Rosa is wise, compassionate, and confident. She can get so caught up in caring for others that she forgets to take care of herself.

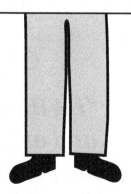

Police Officer Camilla knows a lot about People Safety and teaches people how to protect themselves from harm.

Join Us In Making The
Fullpower Put Safety First Commitment!

"I WILL put the safety and well-being of myself and others ahead of anyone's embarrassment, inconvenience, or offense—including my own!"

 A publication of Kidpower Teenpower Fullpower International® www.kidpower.org For permission to copy, contact safety@kidpower.org

Fullpower Means: Put Safety First!

Put Safety First by paying attention, speaking up, moving away from trouble, and getting help.

1. Safety First means telling people when they hurt your feelings.

2. Safety First means walking away from trouble even when someone is rude.

3. Safety First means using your awareness both to enjoy the world and to watch out for trouble.

4. Safety First means noticing when a fight is about to happen.

5. Safety First means reporting a problem even if you are embarrassed.

A publication of Kidpower Teenpower Fullpower International® www.kidpower.org For permission to copy, contact safety@kidpower.org

7

The Fullpower Underlying Principle

Your safety and well-being are more important than anyone's embarrassment, inconvenience, or offense.

1. Safety First means walking farther to go the safest way home.

2. Safety First means asking someone to go with you, even if you wish you didn't have to.

3. Safety First means speaking up if you don't like the way someone is treating you.

4. Safety First means that your right to say "Please stop" is more important than someone else's feelings.

 A publication of Kidpower Teenpower Fullpower International® www.kidpower.org For permission to copy, contact safety@kidpower.org

Showing Awareness, Calm & Respectful Confidence

Acting with awareness, calm, respect, and confidence help you take charge of your safety!

1. Talib is not aware. This is less safe.

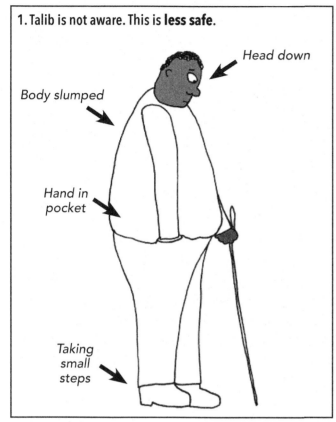

Head down

Body slumped

Hand in pocket

Taking small steps

2. Talib is aware. This is more safe.

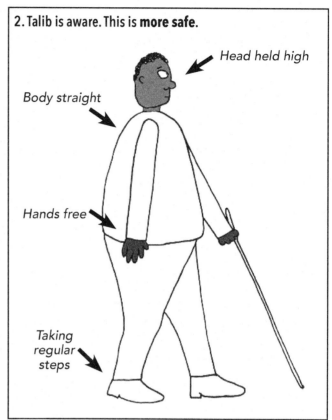

Head held high

Body straight

Hands free

Taking regular steps

3. Mei Lin is not aware. This is less safe.

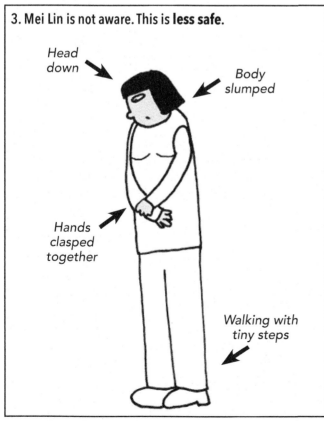

Head down

Body slumped

Hands clasped together

Walking with tiny steps

4. Mei Lin is aware. This is more safe.

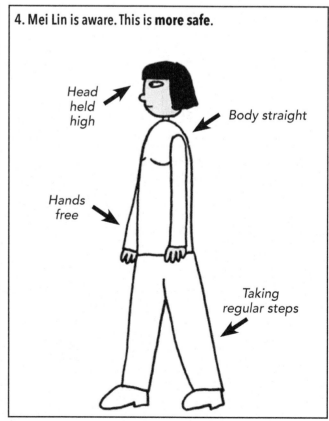

Head held high

Body straight

Hands free

Taking regular steps

Ways Of Acting More And Less Safe

People will listen to you better and bother you less
if you act with awareness, calm, and respectful confidence.

1. An attacker is looking for someone to bother. Mei Lin is not paying attention. Being lost in her own thoughts makes Mei Lin **less safe**.

2. Mei Lin looks around and uses her awareness so nobody can sneak up on her. Being aware makes Mei Lin **more safe**.

3. There is a creepy drunk guy on the street. Rosa starts acting scared. Showing fear makes Rosa **less safe**.

4. Even though Rosa feels afraid on the inside, she decides to act confident and aware as she moves quickly and calmly away to a safer place. This choice helps Rosa to stay **more safe**.

5. Mike yells at some men who are staring at him and being rude. They get mad back. Acting upset makes things **less safe** for Mike.

6. Even though Mike feels furious on the inside, he decides to stay calm and leave confidently and respectfully. This choice helps Mike to stay **more safe**.

 A publication of Kidpower Teenpower Fullpower International® www.kidpower.org For permission to copy, contact safety@kidpower.org

Different Ways To Be Powerful

You can feel one way—and decide to act another. You can choose
to make wise and respectful choices no matter how you feel inside.

1. Mike is mad because his cousin drops his cell phone. He uses his **Mouth Closed Power** instead of saying something rude.

2. Mei Lin feels like hitting the rude guy. She uses her **Hands Down Power** instead.

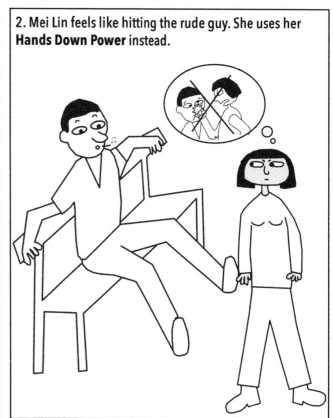

3. Rosa feels like falling asleep. She uses her **Listening Power** instead.

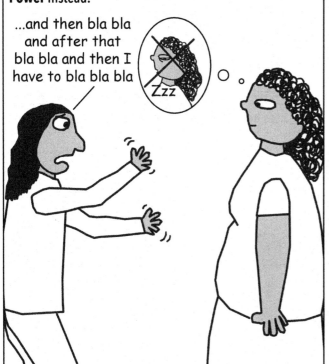

4. Talib feels scared and angry but acts calm. He uses his **Walk Away Power** to get away.

Mei Lin Uses Her Walk Away Power

Getting into a fight with a rude person usually
makes the problem bigger, rather than better.

1. Mei Lin is proud of who she is. She treats others with respect and expects people to be respectful to her.

2. Mei Lin gets angry when people are rude to her.

3. Real fights are dangerous.

4. Real fights get you into trouble, especially if you start them.

5. Next time someone is rude, Mei Lin remembers her **Trash Can.**

6. She uses her **Walk Away Power** to stay safe.

 A publication of Kidpower Teenpower Fullpower International® www.kidpower.org For permission to copy, contact safety@kidpower.org

Mei Lin Protects Herself From Being Pushed

Moving out of reach stops most trouble before it starts.
If it doesn't work, you can set firm and respectful boundaries.

1. A guy at Mei Lin's school pushes people all the time. He does it when he is irritated. He does it when he is showing off. His behavior makes people nervous.

2. Mei Lin walks too close. He calls her a rude word and tries to push her. She wants to hit him and say something mean back. Mei Lin remembers her Walk Away Power, her Hands Down Power, and her Mouth Closed Power. She says nothing and moves out of the way.

Look where you're going, you stupid B#*%@!

3. Mei Lin uses her Walk Away Power to leave. She uses her Imagination Trash Can to throw away the rude word.

4. Next time, Mei Lin moves in a big circle around the guy. She Moves Out of Reach so that he cannot push her.

5. The guy tries to push Mei Lin. She makes a fence with her hands and tells him in a strong big voice, "NO PUSHING!" He stops.

NO PUSHING!

6. Mei Lin gets help from her teacher. The guy who was pushing is embarrassed and gets into trouble. After that, he leaves Mei Lin alone.

TEACHERS' ROOM

Together Or On Your Own

Your safety is different when you are together with
people who can help you—or when you are on your own.

1. Mei Lin is waiting in line for a movie. There are lots of people around.

2. A man is offering coupons for free ice cream. Mei Lin looks around and sees she is together with lots of people. She feels safe taking a coupon.

3. The movie is over, and Mei Lin is waiting for her ride. There is no one around. The man with the coupons comes to offer her more.

4. Mei Lin realizes she is now on her own. She moves away. If she starts to feel uncomfortable, she can go back inside the theater where other people are.

 A publication of Kidpower Teenpower Fullpower International® www.kidpower.org For permission to copy, contact safety@kidpower.org

Know Your Safety Plan

Make safety plans for the different places you go and different situations you are in. Here are some safety plans for the Fullpower Friends. What are your safety plans?

1. A guy bothers Talib on the bus. Talib's Safety Plan is to get out of the guy's way. If the guy keeps bothering him, Talib's Safety Plan is to ask the driver for help.

2. Rosa gets lost at the park. Her Safety Plan is to stand still and look around. If she can't see her friends, she goes to the snack bar, where someone is working. She asks the worker to call her friend who has a mobile phone.

3. Mike is waiting for his ride. He will wait awhile, but maybe the car broke down. Mike can call his friend Joe for a ride if he needs to.

4. There's a new student who keeps grabbing things from Mei Lin. Mei Lin will tell her to stop. If the student does not listen, Mei Lin's Safety Plan is to get help from her teacher. Maybe she can sit next to somebody else.

5. Talib feels a little uncomfortable about a guy who is selling magazines. Talib's Safety Plan is to Think First. No one else is around, so he decides to go into his house.

6. Mei Lin does not open the door to strangers unless she is expecting them, even if it is the pizza person. If someone else is home, she can ask if they ordered pizza.

Personal Information

Personal Information is information about where you live, work, or go to school; what your name is; and other things that are personal about you and your family.

1. Think First before giving personal information to anyone you don't know well.

2. If a stranger asks you for personal information, you can change the subject, choose not to say anything, or move away and get help if you are worried.

3. Remember people you meet online are still strangers. People can pretend to be anybody when they are writing or talking online.

4. It can be okay to give out some personal information if you Think First about whether you have a good reason. Talk with people you trust about when are the times it makes sense to give out personal information.

 A publication of Kidpower Teenpower Fullpower International® www.kidpower.org For permission to copy, contact safety@kidpower.org

Rosa Keeps Herself Safe On The Bus

If someone bothers you, move away. If that doesn't work, get help.

Rosa Thinks First Before She Changes Her Plan

Even with people you know well, before you change your plan, Think First.
Tell people who care about you know who you are with and where you are going.

1. Every day, Rosa waits for the bus to go to school. Sometimes it takes forever for the bus to get there.

2. A car drives up and stops with a man who looks familiar to Rosa. She thinks he is coming to catch the bus.

Thanks for the ride!

3. The man is Pete. Pete was one of Rosa's friends at her old school when she was younger.

Hi Rosa! It's me, Pete! Do you remember me from our old school?

Hi Pete! Yes, I remember you!

4. Pete does not like to wait for the bus. Rosa does not like to wait either. She wishes the bus would come on time.

The bus looks like it is late **again** today. Aren't you tired of waiting?

Yes! I am!

5. Pete says his friend will drive them to school. Rosa says that her plan is to take the bus, even if she has to wait.

My friend says he will drive us to school.

Sorry, but my plan is to take the bus.

6. Pete finds out that the bus isn't coming. Rosa decides to tell her housemate that she will be riding with Pete's friend.

Rosa, my friend just heard on the radio that the bus isn't coming today. You'll be late.

Think First!

Thanks. I will be right back.

A publication of Kidpower Teenpower Fullpower International® www.kidpower.org For permission to copy, contact safety@kidpower.org

Think First Before Opening The Door

When you open your door, you make it easier for someone to bother you.

---

1. Public safety experts recommend that people think carefully before they open their doors to talk to someone or let that person in.

If someone comes to your door who you are not expecting, Think First before you open that door! I've known people who got robbed or hurt because they didn't follow this safety rule.

He seemed so nice and then he took all my money!

---

2. Rosa likes pizza and feels bad for the pizza delivery person, but she Thinks First. She is home alone and no one told her about ordering pizza.

Pizza delivery!

Wrong house. We didn't order pizza today.

---

3. Talib would like to give money to people collecting for charity, but he Thinks First and realizes he doesn't know who these people really are. He gives to charity through organizations he knows.

We are your neighbors collecting for flood victims. Please open the door.

Thank you for your good work, but we never give money at the door. Leave literature outside, and I'll check out your website.

---

4. Mike feels really sorry for his neighbor outside, but he Thinks First and knows that getting her out of the house could be a big problem if she starts acting unsafely.

Please let me in. I need help.

Tell me what you need, and I'll call someone to help you.

The Fullpower Friends At The Park

People you see all the time can still be strangers or acquaintances, so they are not people you know well. Tell people who care about you before you go with them.

1. It is normal to have scary pictures in our minds about strangers.

A stranger is just someone we don't know well. Here at the park, we are strangers to these people, and they are strangers to us. Most people are good even if we don't know each other.

I'm afraid of strangers!

Stranger Danger!

If I see a stranger, I am going to hit him before he hits me!

2. Even familiar, interesting, and friendly people can still be strangers.

We see that clown here all the time. He is nice to kids. Is he still a stranger?

The clown seems really nice but no one here knows him really well. It is ok for those kids to get balloons from him because they are with their adults, but not to go somewhere else with him.

3. Knowing when to stop treating someone like a stranger is complicated.

So when does somebody stop being a stranger and start being somebody we know?

It takes both time and information to get to know someone. Do we know where people live? Their names? Their friends or family? Where they work or go to school?

4. The Fullpower Friends have a great time at the park.

We don't need to be afraid of strangers. We just need to remember how to be safe with strangers.

 A publication of Kidpower Teenpower Fullpower International® www.kidpower.org For permission to copy, contact safety@kidpower.org

Talib's New Phone

You are more important than your things. If someone is trying to hurt
you to get your stuff, it is safer to give it to the person and go and get help.

1. Talib is very proud of his new phone. It is very cool and can do lots of stuff.

WOW!

OH it's so cool!

2. Everybody wants to play with Talib's phone. Talib says that it is his phone. His friends can admire it but they cannot borrow it.

Can I borrow it?

No. It's MY phone. You can look.

Can I try it?!

Just a little while...

3. Two mean guys want to steal Talib's phone. He does not want to lose his phone.

Give us your phone!

But it is MY phone!

Or we'll hurt you!

4. Talib remembers that he is more important than his phone. He gives it to the mean guys. He is sad but he does not want to fight over his property.

Let's split!

Okay. I don't want any trouble.

Great! Now we better run!

5. Talib reports what happened to a police officer. He feels bad about losing his phone. Sometimes making the safest choice is really hard.

...and then they ran away!

You did the right thing! You are more important than your stuff!

POLICE

6. For Talib's birthday, his friends buy him a new phone.

HAPPY BIRTHDAY!!!

Thinking First In Emergencies

If the emergency is happening to you, get help even from a stranger. If the emergency is happening to someone else, Think First about your safest choice.

1. Mike just got bumped by a car. He has to go with strangers in an ambulance. This emergency is happening to Mike.

2. A stranger asks Mike for help. Mike Thinks First and remembers that this is still a stranger. He goes to the store to get help.

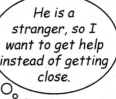

3. Mei Lin is lost in the woods. She hears some strangers calling her name. This emergency is happening to Mei Lin.

4. A woman Mei Lin does not know asks Mei Lin to help find her lost puppy. Mei Lin Thinks First and decides to get help instead of going with a stranger.

5. Talib's house is on fire. A firefighter wearing a mask is banging on the door. This emergency is happening to Talib.

6. An upset woman says her car is on fire. Talib remembers that this woman is a stranger so, he goes to get help from the store.

 A publication of Kidpower Teenpower Fullpower International® www.kidpower.org For permission to copy, contact safety@kidpower.org

The Friends Are At The Mall

Sometimes you have to be very persistent in order to get the help you need.

1. Mei Lin, Rosa, Mike and Talib all go to the shopping mall to see the stores.

2. Some mean people start to yell at them. They use their Walk Away Power and their Roll Away Power.

3. The friends follow their Safety Plan and go into the clothing store to get help.

4. The friends ask for help but the store clerk does not want to get involved.

5. The friends keep asking, but the store clerk tells them to get out of the store.

6. Because it is not safe to leave the store, the friends persist in asking the store clerk to help them. When people who are supposed to help do not listen, sometimes you have to be very firm.

STOP! I NEED HELP!

If someone is scaring you or acting unsafely, you can tell
this person to STOP! You can quickly leave and go get help.

1. A guy who bullies others at school says he is going to beat Mike up. Mike yells "STOP!" and makes a wall with his hands.

2. Mike hurries to his teacher for help. She will help him.

3. A woman at work is mad at Rosa. She uses a rude word and acts scary. Rosa yells, "STOP!" and makes a wall with her hands. The woman stops, and Rosa leaves.

4. Rosa hurries to her boss for help. He says he will help her.

5. A mean guy on the street acts like he is going to hurt Talib. Talib yells "STOP!" He makes a wall with one hand and holds onto his cane with the other hand. The mean guy stops and Talib leaves.

6. Talib hurries to a police officer for help. The police officer says that he will help Talib.

 A publication of Kidpower Teenpower Fullpower International® www.kidpower.org For permission to copy, contact safety@kidpower.org

Mei Lin Gets Away From Trouble

The Arm Grab Escape can help you get away from someone who is grabbing you without having to hurt that person.

1. Mei Lin is walking home. There are some men who are whistling at her and making comments about how she looks.

2. One of the guys grabs her arm.

3. Mei Lin grabs her own arm, and pulls away, yelling, "NO!" The guys who are bothering her are very surprised! She walks away quickly with awareness.

4. Mei Lin is going to tell her mother what happened right away.

Introduction To Boundaries

A boundary is like a fence. It sets a limit. Personal boundaries are the limits between people. We have to set boundaries with ourselves and with each other.

The rules about personal boundaries are:

1. We each belong to ourselves. You belong to you, and I belong to me. This means that your body belongs to you—and so does your personal space, your feelings, your time, your thoughts—all of you! This means that other people belong to themselves too. For example, touch or games for fun or for affection should be the choice of each person, safe, and allowed by the people in charge.

2. Some things are not a choice. This is true for adults as well as for young people. For example, unwanted touch is sometimes necessary because of your health and safety.

3. Problems should not be secrets. Anything that bothers you, me, or anybody else should not have to be a secret, even if it makes someone upset or embarrassed. Presents, favors, games, visits, photos, videos, and touch should also not have to be kept secret.

4. Keep telling until you get help. When you have a problem, find an adult you trust who has enough authority to help you, and keep on telling until you get the help you need. It is never too late to tell!

1. We each belong to ourselves.

2. Some things are not a choice.

I hate when you do that. It hurts!

Sorry, I have to do it to help you feel better.

3. Problems should not be secrets.

Please don't tell!

I will help you talk with your parents.

4. Keep telling until you get help.

He's bothering me!

I will help you.

 A publication of Kidpower Teenpower Fullpower International® www.kidpower.org For permission to copy, contact safety@kidpower.org

Speak Up Power And Listening Power

Others cannot read your mind, so tell them if something
they do starts to bother you—and listen when they tell you.

1. Sometimes when Mei Lin is happy, she punches Talib's arm. She does not know that it hurts Talib.

2. People who care about you need to know if something they say or do hurts you.

3. Mike loves to give back rubs. Sometimes Rosa does not like it.

4. It is okay to like a back rub one day and change your mind on a different day.

5. Mike usually likes Talib's jokes, but this time the joke hurts Mike's feelings.

6. Speak up if some kinds of jokes make you feel uncomfortable or embarrassed.

The Trash Can Technique

Protect your feelings from negative messages by throwing
away hurtful words. Replace unkind messages with positive self-talk.

1. Mei Lin catches the words "Shut Up!" and throws them into a real trash can. She gives herself a positive message to take in.

The Real Trash Can

2. People of all ages use the Kidpower Trash Can technique. Mike puts one hand on a hip and imagines that the hole it makes is his personal trash can. He uses his other hand to catch a hurting word and then throws it into his trash can.

Fullpower Trash Can

3. Rosa makes a Mini Trash Can by curling up her fingers on one hand. She pushes the word "Stupid" into the little hole her hand makes with her thumb to throw it away.

Mini Trash Can

4. Rosa uses her mind to throw the word "Fat" into her Imagination Trash Can. She uses positive self-talk to replace the hurtful message.

Imagination Trash Can

 A publication of Kidpower Teenpower Fullpower International® www.kidpower.org For permission to copy, contact safety@kidpower.org

Talib Learns To Protect His Feelings

Get support from people who care about you if
you feel badly about what someone said or did to you.

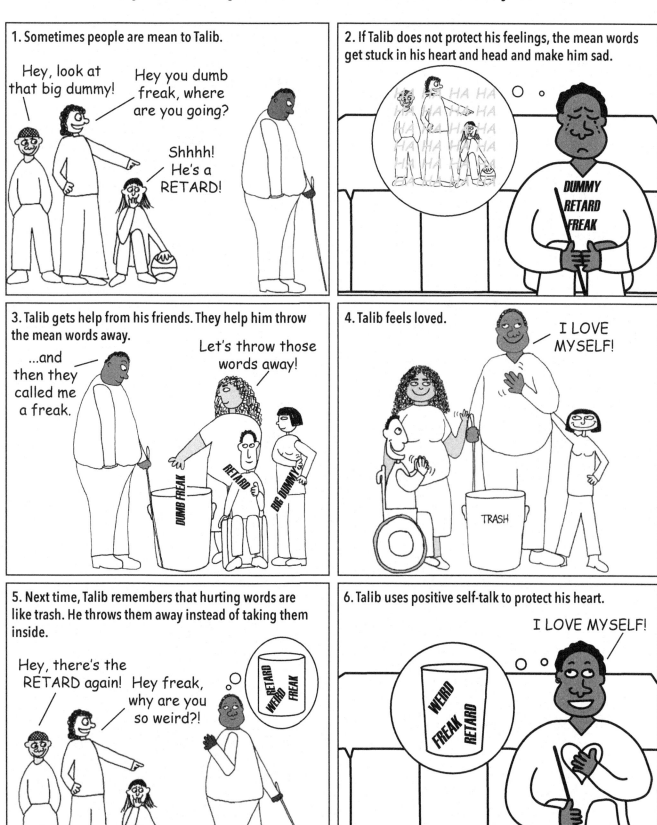

Accepting Compliments

If someone says one positive thing to you and one
negative thing, what are you most likely to remember?

1. It can be hard to take in compliments. Talib throws away the nice things Mike says.

2. Sometimes Mei Lin has trouble taking in compliments too.

3. Officer Camilla explains that taking in kind messages is like eating healthy, delicious food—it will help you to stay well and feel good.

4. Talib accepts his compliment from Mike.

5. Mei Lin accepts her compliment from Rosa.

 A publication of Kidpower Teenpower Fullpower International® www.kidpower.org For permission to copy, contact safety@kidpower.org

Throw Away Insults, Not Information

When people are upset, sometimes they speak up in ways that are unkind.
We can separate the hurtful parts of their messages from the parts that are important.

1. Rosa missed class and would like to borrow Mike's notes. Mike doesn't want to let Rosa have them, because she lost them last time.

Can I borrow your notes from class?

NO, you can't have them! Last time I gave you my notes you lost them. You are such a slob!

2. Rosa realizes Mike is giving her some useful information. She throws away the insult and takes in the information.

Telling me that I need to be more careful with things I borrow is useful information. Calling me a slob is an insult. I promise to give your notes right back.

Okay, thanks. Sorry for calling you a slob.

3. Talib is enjoying listening to music. His mom is frustrated with him because it has taken him so long to come down for dinner.

Talib, this is the third time I have told you to come down to dinner. You are so lazy!

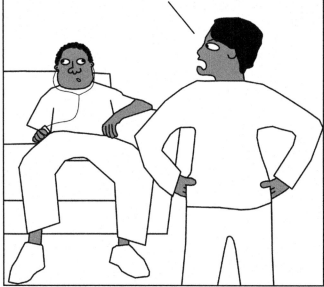

4. Talib realizes he needs to listen better when his parents are talking to him. He takes in the useful information and throws away the insulting word, "lazy."

Telling me to come down to dinner is useful information, even if I want to finish what I am listening to. Calling me lazy is insulting.

You're right. I am sorry for calling you lazy, and it is important to me that you come down to dinner when I ask you to.

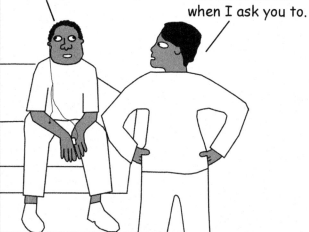

"That's Not True!" Power

If someone combines something that is true about you with something that is unkind and untrue, protect yourself by making a fence with your hands and say, "That's not true!"

1. Rosa is going to pretend to be mean to help Mei Lin to practice being safe with her feelings.

I am pretending so we can practice. I am going to put something that is true with something that is not true.

Okay!

2. It is true that Mei Lin is short. It is NOT true that Mei Lin is weak. Mei Lin is strong and powerful!

You are WEAK because you are short!

THAT'S NOT TRUE!

3. Mei Lin and Rosa switch roles for who is pretending to be mean.

I am pretending to be very mean so we can practice.

Okay!

4. It is true that Rosa is round instead of thin. It is NOT true that Rosa is ugly. Rosa is beautiful both inside and outside!

You are UGLY because you are fat!

THAT'S NOT TRUE!

 A publication of Kidpower Teenpower Fullpower International® www.kidpower.org For permission to copy, contact safety@kidpower.org

More "That's Not True!" Situations

Practicing protecting yourself from unkind things others say, or you say to yourself, can prepare you to do this in real life. Remind each other that you are pretending.

1. Mike is going to pretend to be mean to help Talib to practice being safe with his feelings.

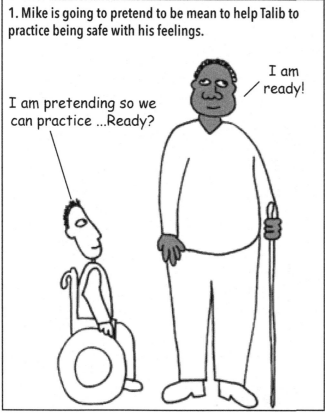

2. It is true that Talib is visually impaired and cannot see so well. It is NOT true that Talib is awful. Talib is wonderful and a really great person.

3. Talib is going to pretend to be mean so Mike can practice protecting his feelings.

4. It is true that Mike uses a wheelchair. It is NOT true that Mike is useless. Mike is very important and can do lots of things.

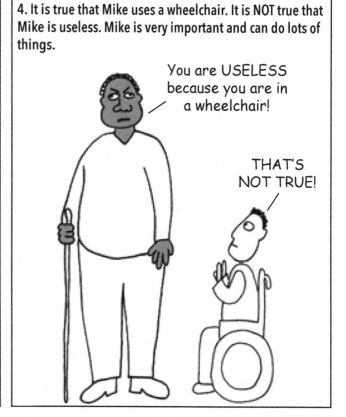

Safety Rules On Touch

Touch, games, problems, photos, presents someone
gives you, and activities should not have to be secret.

1. Touch for health and safety is often not a choice.

If you are about to hit somebody, being stopped is not a choice. If you are badly hurt, you may have to go to the doctor.

2. Touch of any kind should never ever have to be a secret—whether you like it or not and whether it is a choice or not.

Problems should not be secrets. Any kind of touch that bothers you should **not** have to be a secret.

3. Suppose someone crosses and breaks the safety rules. You can say, "Stop or else!" "I will leave!" "You have to leave!" "I'll report you!"

Stop or else!

4. An unsafe bribe is when someone tries to give you something to get you to lower your boundaries and do something unsafe, dishonest, or unkind.

If someone offers you an unsafe bribe, they are breaking the safety rules. You can say, "Stop or I'll leave," or, "Stop or you'll have to leave," or, "Stop or I'll tell."

Stop or I will tell!

 A publication of Kidpower Teenpower Fullpower International® www.kidpower.org For permission to copy, contact safety@kidpower.org

When Someone Breaks The Safety Rules

You can tell someone to leave if this person is in your space. You can decide to leave if you are in another space. You can get help by making a report.

1. Another way to break the safety rules is if someone uses his or her power in a wrong way.

2. Your private areas are the parts of your body covered by a bathing suit.

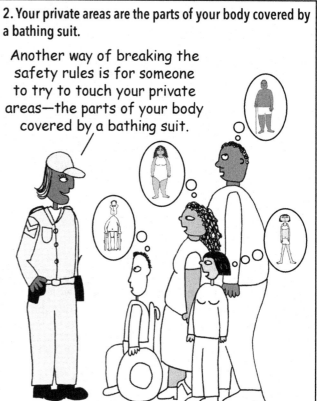

3. The safety rule is, except for health or safety, people should not touch your private areas, ask you to touch their private areas, or show you pictures of people doing this.

4. As you grow up, the safety rules about touching private areas can change. Talk with your families or adult support people about your rules and values.

Rosa Sets Firm Boundaries

Sometimes you have to be very persistent in setting boundaries with people you know.

1. A friend of Rosa's named Abel keeps touching her arm and trying to hold her hand.

2. Rosa likes Abel, but she does not want to hold hands. She looks at him, gives him back his hand, and tells him to stop.

3. Abel does not listen so Rosa makes a fence with her hands. She makes sure she sounds and looks like she means it when she tells him to stop.

4. Abel's feelings are hurt. Rosa still sets a clear boundary. You can be friends and not hold hands.

5. Rosa does not hold hands for a computer. She knows that this unsafe bribe crosses the line.

6. When Abel gets angry, Rosa feels scared. She knows it is okay to lie and break a promise IF you are doing it to be safe AND you get help as soon as you can.

 A publication of Kidpower Teenpower Fullpower International® www.kidpower.org For permission to copy, contact safety@kidpower.org

Rosa Tells To Get Help

If you have a safety problem, get help from an adult you trust
as quickly as you can. Keep asking until you get the help you need.

1. After she is away from Abel, Rosa decides that the person who can help her the most is her mother.

It is OK to tell a lie and break a promise to stay safe and because I am going to tell someone in charge right away.

2. Rosa tells her mother that she has a problem. Her mother is busy on the computer and does not understand what Rosa says.

Excuse me, Mom! I have a problem.

That's nice honey! I am glad you had a good day...

3. Rosa asks her mother to listen to her. Her mother has had a hard day and gets angry.

MOM! Please listen to me!

WHAT IS IT? CAN'T I GET A MINUTE'S PEACE?

4. Rosa knows that it is okay to interrupt her mother and keep asking for help if she has a Safety Problem.

But I have a Safety Problem!

Oh! This is about your safety! Please tell me what happened.

5. Rosa tells her mother that Abel did not listen. But her mother does not understand. Rosa's mother cannot read Rosa's mind.

Abel was not listening to me!

You interrupted me for THAT! That's NOT a Safety Problem. You two ALWAYS argue!

6. Rosa tells her mom the whole story. Her mother will help her.

But, he wanted to hold my hand, and I told him to stop. He didn't listen, and then he tried to bribe me. He got angry and told me not to tell.

Thank you for telling me. I'm sorry I yelled at you. We will figure out what to do.

A publication of Kidpower Teenpower Fullpower International® www.kidpower.org For permission to copy, contact safety@kidpower.org

Talib Keeps Asking Until He Gets Help

Be persistent until you find someone who is
willing to listen and do something to solve your problem.

1. Talib is walking to the bus stop at his school. Another student starts to bully him by grabbing his backpack.

2. Talib uses his Stop Power and yells "NO." He uses his Walk Away Power to go find a safer place to be.

3. The student bullying Talib keeps following him and saying cruel things. Talib protects his feelings.

4. Talib goes to the principal's office for help, but the principal is too busy to listen.

5. Talib goes to the janitor, but today she is very busy and having a bad day.

6. Talib meets his favorite teacher in the hall and gets help so he can be safe.

A publication of Kidpower Teenpower Fullpower International® www.kidpower.org For permission to copy, contact safety@kidpower.org

What Is Bullying & What Can You Do About It?

We all have the right to be safe and respected—and the
responsibility to act safely and respectfully towards others.

1. Bullying happens when someone uses his or her power on purpose to hurt you, scare you, or make you feel bad.

2. No one should have to face bullying alone.

3. Threatening to hurt someone is bullying.

4. Mike can leave and then ask for help.

5. Tripping, shoving, or laughing at someone is bullying.

6. Talib can get his balance, move away, set a boundary, and leave.

Take Charge To Stay Safe From Bullying

Find other people to hang out with, speak up, and protect your feelings.

1. Leaving someone out is bullying.

2. Mei Lin can find someone else to talk to.

3. Trying to make other people not like someone is bullying.

4. Speaking up can prevent problems from getting bigger.

5. Making fun of people is bullying.

6. Mike and Mei Lin can throw hurtful words away and say something nice to themselves.

 A publication of Kidpower Teenpower Fullpower International® www.kidpower.org For permission to copy, contact safety@kidpower.org

Stop Others From Bullying

We can work together to create caring, respect, and safety for everyone, everywhere.

1. Don't agree with hurtful teasing or jokes. Tell people to respect differences.

2. If someone is being left out, go talk with that person.

3. If someone is being hurt or threatened, speak up if you can do it safely.

4. If someone tries to make you feel bad about someone else, ask why and say that you don't listen to gossip.

5. People should be safe at school, at work, at home, and in their communities. Report problems like people being hurt, threatened, made fun of, or left out.

Talib Gets Bullied At Work

If someone is picking on you and calling you
names, it is normal to feel alone and like it is your fault.

1. There is a guy at work named JoJo who lots of people like. Talib does not like JoJo because JoJo is always picking on him and calling him names.

2. JoJo is always poking Talib and putting him down.

3. In the lunch room, JoJo knocks Talib's tray over on purpose.

4. JoJo tells Talib that he will get him fired and beat him up if he tells. Talib promises not to tell.

 A publication of Kidpower Teenpower Fullpower International® www.kidpower.org For permission to copy, contact safety@kidpower.org

Talib Takes Charge Of His Safety

If you know someone is being bullied at work, at school, or in your community, speak up if you can do so safely—and reach out to offer support.

Staying Safe Online

Think First before sharing private information through the Internet or mobile technology, even if it seems secure.

---

1. Online technology is great because it can make communication easier.

2. The people you meet on the Internet are strangers to you. Check and Think First before you give out personal information, even on semi-secure sites like YouTube and Facebook. Make a Safety Plan before you meet or talk to anyone you get to know via the Internet.

3. The Internet is a great way to learn many things, but not everything you find on it is true. Double-check the source on any sites to make sure you are getting accurate information.

4. Some information on the Internet may not be appropriate to view at work, school, or in certain families.

 A publication of Kidpower Teenpower Fullpower International® www.kidpower.org For permission to copy, contact safety@kidpower.org

Prevent Cyber-Bullying

Cyber-bullying happens when people use technology to be hurtful to someone, such as mobile phones, chat rooms, gaming environments, and social media.

1. Don't post or write anything on the Internet that you don't want the world to see. This is true for e-mails, social networks, and instant messages as well as text messages and digital photos on mobile phones. You want to be very careful what you write, say, and do, as it can get passed around to lots of people quickly.

2. When people misuse technology to bully others, it is called cyber-bullying. Cyber-bullying is against the law. Think about whether what you are doing might be hurtful or embarrassing to someone.

Welcome Rosa! You are now logged in.

Haha! Wouldn't it be funny to write something about Rosa and see how surprised she would be! But that might be embarrassing for her... so I shouldn't do it.

3. Speak up if you see anyone cyber-bullying and tell them that it is wrong. Get help from other people you trust, if you need to.

Whoa... you should see what a bad picture I got of Rosa! I should send it out to all our friends.

We shouldn't do something that would hurt or upset her, even if it seems funny to us.

4. If someone does bully you over the Internet or with a text message or photo on a mobile phone, don't delete the message. Save it, print it if you can, don't reply, and get help to report what happened!

OH NO! That guy from the soccer game is really mad at me. He is saying he is going to tell everyone horrible things about me.

Save the e-mail and don't write back. We can talk to our parents and coach about what happened. And if things get worse, we can tell Officer Camilla.

Resisting Peer Pressure
There are lots of different ways to say "NO."

Thank you to family counselor Sharon Scott, LPC, PMFT for permission to incorporate ideas from her peer pressure reversal skills program into our curriculum. Sharon is the author of the best-selling book, How to Say NO and Keep Your Friends (HRD Press, 1997, 800-822-2801 http://www.hrdpress.com/Sharon Scott)

1. Rosa is visiting a cousin who is mad at the neighbor. Rosa knows that putting toilet paper all over the house and yard will get them in trouble. Rosa acts shocked so her cousin will know that they are not going to toilet paper the neighbor's house.

Hey, Rosa, I'm really mad at my neighbor. Let's go toilet paper her home.

ARE YOU KIDDING? WE'LL BE GROUNDED FOREVER IF WE DO THAT!

2. Mei Lin is at a sleepover at her friend's house. Her friend wants to sneak out late at night. Mei Lin knows this is not safe. So she has a better idea and they watch a movie.

I'm bored. Everybody here is asleep. Let's sneak out and go downtown...

I have a better idea. Let's watch the movie we rented. We already paid for it!

3. A friend of Mike's is always saying mean things about other people. There is a new student who Mike's friend makes fun of. Mike changes the subject by telling the guy that the new student thinks he is nice, even though she did not say anything. Maybe that will stop his friend from being mean.

You know what I think? That new girl is really gross. Let's tell everyone to stay away from her...

Well, guess what she said about YOU! She said that YOU'RE really NICE!

4. Mike's neighbor tries to get him to help steal at the store. Mike knows that stealing is wrong. He tells his neighbor he likes him too much to steal.

Hey Mike, you distract the cashier by buying this soda, and I'll steal us some candy bars.

I really like you a lot, but stealing is wrong and could get us into lots of trouble. It's not worth it.

More Ways To Resist Peer Pressure

Instead of following someone who is acting in a hurtful or
dangerous way, you can be a leader for safety and respect.

1. The teacher has said that the next person who talks
in class will get a bad grade. The girl next to Mei Lin is
always talking. Mei Lin does not want to get in trouble so
she ignores her by pretending that she does not hear.

Hey, Mei Lin, guess what I heard at a party
yesterday. Psst. Psst. What's WITH you?!

2. Another student tries to get Rosa to cut class. Rosa does
not want to miss class. She interrupts the student and
leaves to go to class.

Hey, Rosa, that
substitute is so
stupid she'll never
notice we're missing.
Let's cut class...

No thanks! I've
got to go...

3. A friend at a party wants to take embarrassing photos
with Talib's mobile phone. Talib knows that texting
photos like these can be hurtful. He makes a silly joke to
let this person know he thinks it is a bad idea.

Let's take a photo of
that girl when she's
not looking and send
it to everybody.

My phone is much too
smart to do anything
that might upset her.

4. Talib's neighbor wants to show him a gun. Talib knows
that fooling around with guns can be dangerous. He
makes an excuse so he can leave quickly.

I'm sorry. I forgot that
I'm supposed to meet my
mom. I'm late! Gotta go!

Hey Talib, my
housemate
got a gun for
protection. It's
right here in
this drawer...

Safe And Unsafe Friends

Safe friends treat you with respect. It is important to tell people in a calm and clear way when something is okay with you and when it is not.

1. Mike's neighbor wants to borrow money from him, but he forgets to pay it back. Mike needs his money.

2. Mike's neighbor is angry and says mean things. Mike throws those words away and says that good friends pay back money when they borrow it.

3. Rosa's housemate wants to bring people over who make trouble. Rosa says that they cannot come in because last time they caused a lot of problems.

4. Rosa's housemate is angry and says mean things. Rosa throws those words away and says she has to agree about who comes over.

5. Mei Lin's boyfriend wants to stay the night. Mei Lin tells him it is time to go home.

6. Mei Lin's boyfriend is angry and says mean things. Mei Lin throws those words away and says that true boyfriends do not try to pressure their girlfriends.

 A publication of Kidpower Teenpower Fullpower International® www.kidpower.org For permission to copy, contact safety@kidpower.org

The Too-Long Kiss

How long, how often, and when to kiss is often different
for different people, even when they care about each other.

1. Talib and his girlfriend Mira love each other.

2. Talib really likes kissing Mira.

3. Mira doesn't like long kisses in public.

Not right now. You want to kiss too often and too long.

4. Talib's feelings get hurt. Mira explains that she likes little kisses and not getting kissed all the time.

But I thought you loved me!

I do love you, but I don't like to be kissed all the time. And I like short little kisses, not great big ones. Please ask first.

The Joy Of Being Single

Many people are happy living alone.

1. Rosa's mother is single and has a wonderful life.

2. Rosa is worried about her mother being alone.

3. Rosa's grandma is worried too. Rosa and her grandma keep talking to Rosa's mom about getting a boyfriend.

4. Rosa's mom explains to both of them that she is very happy being single and living alone.

A publication of Kidpower Teenpower Fullpower International® www.kidpower.org For permission to copy, contact safety@kidpower.org

The Uncomfortable Photos Story

Speak up if you don't want someone to take your photo.

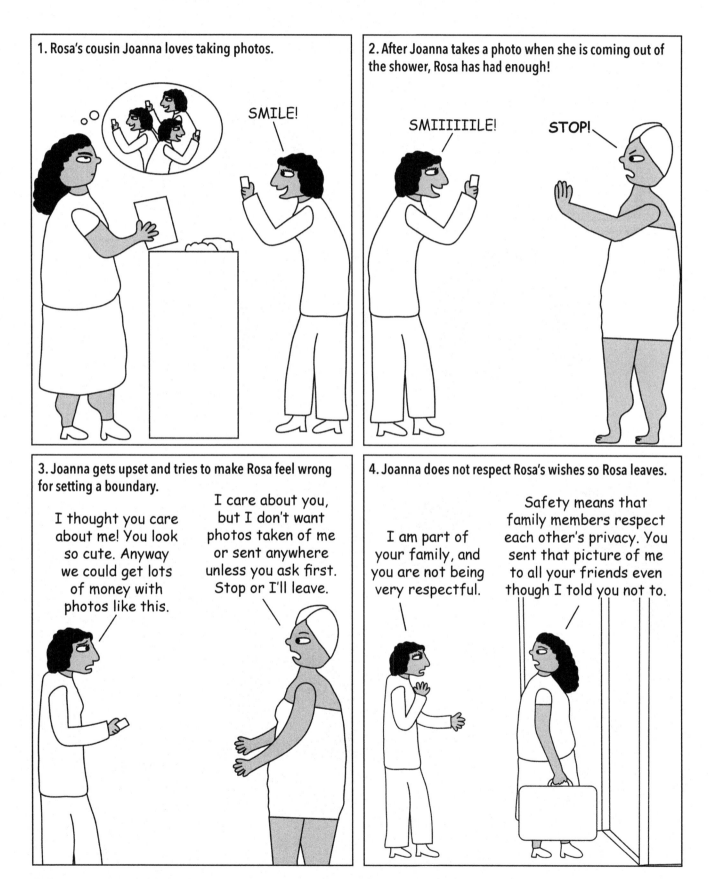

Rosa Gets Cyber-Bullied By Her Cousin Joanna

Sometimes family members act unsafely and disrespectfully.

1. Rosa is shocked by the unkind messages and embarrassing photos that Joanna is texting.

2. Rosa tells her to stop, but Joanna does not listen.

3. Rosa asks her aunt for help.

4. Her aunt decides to stop paying for Joanna's mobile phone until she apologizes.

 A publication of Kidpower Teenpower Fullpower International® www.kidpower.org For permission to copy, contact safety@kidpower.org

Ensuring Consent Can Be Romantic

To stay safe, keep checking to make sure that romantic touch is truly okay with each person, and stop as soon as someone changes their mind.

Rosa And Anna Face Prejudice

Being cruel to people for being different is unsafe and disrespectful.

1. Rosa and her girlfriend, Anna, love each other.

2. Sometimes people say mean things because Rosa and Anna are two women who love each other.

3. Rosa and Anna decide to walk away and get the bus from another bus stop.

4. Rosa speaks up in a respectful way while leaving with Anna to go to safety.

 A publication of Kidpower Teenpower Fullpower International® www.kidpower.org For permission to copy, contact safety@kidpower.org

Rosa And Anna Stand Up Against Prejudice

Being persistent means not giving up even when people don't listen.

1. Rosa and Anna go to the office to report what happened.

It wouldn't have happened if you did not make such a spectacle of yourselves.

They were very threatening and calling us names.

2. The woman in the office is very rude.

Other couples hold hands here. Why can't we?

That is different. You should not call attention to yourselves.

3. Rosa and Anna tell their friends what happened. Their friends are very supportive and help them.

You throw those mean words in the trash. You are both wonderful people and a GREAT COUPLE!

...And then she said we "shouldn't call attention to ourselves."

THAT IS AWFUL!

This is a prejudice problem. Prejudice is against the rules. We need to tell the director.

4. They all go to the director and tell her what happened. She listens, understands, and makes a plan.

I am so sorry that happened to you. Mei Lin is right. We need to teach people here that it is not okay to say mean things about other people or threaten them FOR ANY REASON.

DIRECTOR

The Breakup Story

Dating has to be okay with each person,
but telling someone you want to stop can be very hard.

1. Mike wants to break up with Reba, but he doesn't know how to do it. His friends tell him that he has to tell her even though she will be upset.

I don't want to be Reba's boyfriend anymore. But she's going to be upset. I just tried seeing her less, but her feelings got terribly hurt.

There, there!

It is unkind not to tell Reba. Be clear and kind and respectful.

2. Mike tells Reba as kindly and clearly as he can, but she is still very sad. Breaking up breaks hearts. It is really hard to do.

I think you are a really great person. And it is not working for me anymore to be your boyfriend. I want to break up.

But I love you!

3. Mike wants Reba to be happy, but he cannot be the one to help her.

It was awful! She's calling every night and talking for hours about how upset she is. She keeps asking why. I feel terrible!

How terrible!

You need to tell Reba that she has to find someone else to talk to.

4. Sometimes the best way to help someone is to help them think of others who can help.

How can you do this to me?

I understand that you are really sad, and I'm really sorry. I can't help you, but let's think of someone who you can talk to.

5. Mei Lin can stay friends with both Mike and Reba as long as she sees them separately and stays out of the middle.

I like both Mike and Reba and want to stay friends with both of them.

You can be friends with both but need to see them at different times and places. And not to talk about either of them to each other so that you don't get in the middle.

6. Reba decides to find other people to have fun with. She misses Mike but understands that being a couple has to work well for both people.

 A publication of Kidpower Teenpower Fullpower International® www.kidpower.org For permission to copy, contact safety@kidpower.org

Acting Responsibly

In healthy relationships, people do their best to be understanding and to keep their commitments.

1. Acting responsibly means not doing something in front of people that leaves them feeling left out.

2. Finding things you can enjoy doing together is important in healthy relationships.

3. Acting responsibly means cleaning up after yourself even if you are very busy.

4. Acting responsibly means speaking up when someone is thoughtless–and listening when someone tells you about a problem.

5. Acting responsibly means being on time and keeping your commitments.

6. In healthy relationships, people can count on each other!

Talib Has A Grumpy Day

If someone you care about is being unkind, sometimes
leaving with kindness is the best way to protect everyone's feelings.

1. One night, Talib does not get enough sleep. In the morning, he wakes up in a bad mood.

2. Talib is mean to his friends.

3. Rosa starts to think. Mei Lin gets angry and says something mean back to Talib. Mike is sad and feels bad about himself. Talib gets more grumpy.

4. Rosa decides not to get upset. She makes a Mini Trash Can by curling up her fingers on one hand. She uses her thumb to throw away the words "I hate you!" She replaces these hurting words with positive self-talk.

5. Rosa decides to leave with kindness. She, Mei Lin, Mike, and Talib use their Walk Away Power. Even though he doesn't act like it, Talib takes Rosa's words "we like you a lot" into his heart.

I am sad you said you hate us because we like you a lot. We will talk to you when you are feeling better.

6. After a while, Talib is feeling better. He apologizes to his friends.

I am sorry I said I hate you. It is not true. I was in a bad mood.

A publication of Kidpower Teenpower Fullpower International® www.kidpower.org For permission to copy, contact safety@kidpower.org

Mike Speaks Up

If people are bullying, you might need to try out
different ways of stopping them, while also keeping yourself safe.

1. Mike is talking with some friends. He notices that some kids are bullying a smaller guy. He feels guilty and sad.

2. Mike does not want to have the bullies bother him, but he does want to help the smaller guy. He pretends to see a teacher coming so that the bullies will leave.

3. Mike reaches out to support the smaller guy, whose name is Frank.

4. Mike tells Frank that they need to get help. Frank is afraid. He does not want the bullies to take revenge on them for telling.

5. Mike says that the bullies will bother Frank and other people again if they are not stopped. Frank is worried but he agrees.

6. Mike and Frank talk to Mike's favorite teacher at school. She promises to let the bullies think that she saw what happened so they won't know that Mike and Frank told. She is glad that they came to her for help.

Mike Has Trouble At Home

Violence and threats in families are hurtful to everyone.

1. Mike's mother gets into fights with her boyfriend when they are drinking. Mike is sad when they are fighting.

2. Mike's mother gets knocked down by her boyfriend. Mike is scared that she will get hurt.

3. Mike tires to protect his mother. She is mad and says mean things to him.

4. Mike dreams all night about the fight and the mean things his mother said.

 A publication of Kidpower Teenpower Fullpower International® www.kidpower.org For permission to copy, contact safety@kidpower.org

Mike Gets Help To Be Safer At Home

It can be hard to tell people if you have trouble at home.
But you deserve to have help instead of feeling alone.

1. In the morning, Mike's mother is sorry. He is upset.

2. Mike tells his friends about his problem. His friends give him good advice.

3. Mike talks to a counselor. She tells Mike about his different choices.

4. Next time there is a fight, Mike goes to his room. He knows now that if he thinks someone might get hurt, his Safety Plan is to call 911.

Mei Lin Has Boyfriend Trouble

It is NOT loving to be jealous or insulting—or to hit, push, or grab.

1. When Mei Lin wants to leave a party early, her boyfriend gets jealous. This makes Mei Lin mad.

2. Mei Lin's boyfriend pushes her and says mean things. She tells him she wants to go away from him.

3. Mei Lin's boyfriend grabs her arm hard. It hurts. He says that she cannot leave.

4. Mei Lin pulls her arm away and yells for help.

Mei Lin Gets Away From The Problem Boyfriend

It can be sad to leave someone who is often nice but sometimes hurtful.
In healthy relationships, people treat each other with caring and respect.

1. Mei Lin is sad. Her boyfriend is mad. Her friends want to help.

2. Mei Lin's boyfriend goes away.

3. Mei Lin misses her boyfriend. Her friends tell her that she needs a better boyfriend.

4. Mei Lin meets a new guy. He is really nice. When she wants to go home, he listens.

Protecting Ourselves From Negative Self-Talk

We are safer and happier when we give ourselves positive messages.

1. Sometimes Talib drops things, or makes mistakes. When he drops things, he feels bad about himself and calls himself names.

2. Mike wants Talib to be kind to himself. He reminds him to use positive self-talk.

3. Rosa and Mei Lin are in the bathroom brushing their hair. Rosa doesn't like the way she looks in the mirror. She says mean things to herself.

4. Mei Lin reminds Rosa to be kind to herself. She tells Rosa she is beautiful. Rosa imagines the hurtful words in a trash can inside her head and takes Mei Lin's compliment into her heart.

 A publication of Kidpower Teenpower Fullpower International® www.kidpower.org For permission to copy, contact safety@kidpower.org

More Problems With Negative Self-Talk

Caring friends can be a big help in stopping us from being mean to ourselves.

1. Mike is having a hard time with his homework. He is feeling very frustrated and angry with himself.

2. Talib helps Mike see himself in a more positive way. Mike stops picking on himself.

3. Mei Lin gets frustrated with being short. She can't reach things easily and has a hard time seeing in a crowd.

4. Rosa tells Mei Lin that everyone has things about themselves that they wish they could change. She thinks Mei Lin should enjoy being the way she is. Mei Lin realizes that her friend is right.

The Mean Words Recycling Machine

What we are really doing is recycling the sounds and letters of negative messages and turning them into positive messages we can take into our hearts.

The Fullpower Friends know it is better for the earth to recycle than to throw things away.
They decide that they will start recycling hurtful words and turning them into caring words!

HATE MYSELF!
SO STUPID! UGLY!
FAT! I WISH I
WERE DIFFERENT!
CLUMSY!
TOO SHORT!

I LOVE MYSELF!
I AM PROUD OF
WHO I AM! I AM
BEAUTIUFL! I AM
GREAT! I AM SMART!

A publication of Kidpower Teenpower Fullpower International® www.kidpower.org For permission to copy, contact safety@kidpower.org

kid**power** Protection Promise™
For All Ages And Abilities Everywhere
Imagine the impact if we each discussed this message with everyone
who is important in our lives—and convinced them that we mean it!

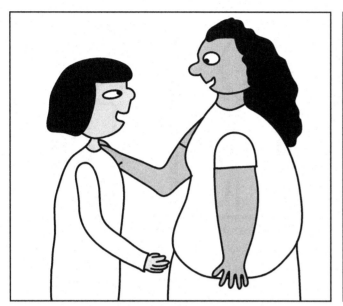 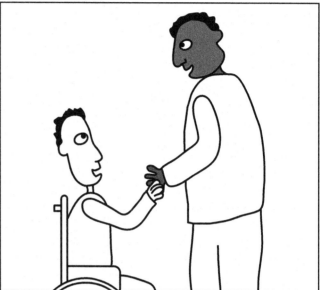

"You are VERY important to me! If you have a safety problem, I want to know. Even if I seem too busy. Or might feel upset. Or don't understand at first. Even if someone we care about will be upset. Even if it is embarrassing. Even if you made a mistake. Please tell me, and I will do everything in my power to help you."

kidpower® Safety Signals for Everyone, Everywhere To Help Prevent And Solve Problems

Safety Signals are simple gestures, drawings, and words to help all of us remember important People Safety ideas and skills.

Wait Power
Hold your own hands to show times when you need to wait patiently to stay safe and be respectful.

Stay Aware Power
Point towards your eyes, turn your head, and look around to signal how to pay attention and act alert.

Stay Together Power
Start with your palms apart and facing outwards, and then move them together to signal staying together to stay safe out in public.

Check First Power
Clasp your forearm with the other hand to show checking first with the adults who care about you before you change your plan.

Think First Power
Pat your head gently to show thinking first about what to do when the unexpected happens or someone is acting unsafely.

Walk Away Power
Use your fingers like legs and walk them on your arm to help you remember to walk away from any person or situation that might be unsafe.

Roll Away Power
Roll your fingers along the other arm to show using wheels to roll away from trouble and get to safety.

Get Help Power
Put your arms in front of you with palms facing up like a bridge to show reaching out to get help or to make a connection.

The full set of Kidpower Safety Signals can be downloaded from our online Library at www.kidpower.org

 A publication of Kidpower Teenpower Fullpower International® www.kidpower.org For permission to copy, contact safety@kidpower.org

kid**power** Safety Signals For Taking Charge Of Our Feelings, Words, And Bodies

The keys to remembering to use People Safety strategies and skills in real life are simplicity, repetition, consistency, fun, and practice.

Calm Down Power

Press your palms together, straighten your back, breathe deeply and slowly, and feel your feet to calm down.

Mouth Closed Power

Squeeze your lips together to stop yourself from doing anything unsafe with what you say or do with your mouth.

Hands And Feet Down Power

Imagine you are about to bother or hurt someone with your hands or feet and then pull them down to your sides or the floor.

Hang On Power

To show stopping yourself from touching or hitting someone, hang onto your sides or pockets.

Speak Up Power

Put your hand in front of your mouth and move it outwards to show speaking up about what you do and do not want.

Fence Power

Put your arms in front of you waist-high with palms facing downwards to show making a fence to set boundaries with someone who is bothering you.

Trash Can Power

Put a hand on your hip and pretend the hole it makes is your personal trash can. Use your other hand to catch hurting words and throw them away.

Heart Power

Reach forward and then press your hands into your chest to show scooping kind words into your heart, protecting your heart, and using your heart to be kind to others.

The full set of Kidpower Safety Signals can be downloaded from our online Library at www.kidpower.org

kidpower® Safety Signals For Healthy Boundaries With People We Know

These Safety Signals help everyone, everywhere remember the boundary rules and principles for staying safe and having fun with people we know.

Safety Signals about the four Kidpower Boundary Rules.

We each belong to ourselves

Point to yourself, sit tall, and smile to show that each person's body, time, feelings, and thoughts are important.

Some things are not a choice

Shrug and smile to show that some things are required, and boundaries often have to be negotiated, even for adults.

Problems should not be secrets

Hold a finger in front of your lips. Now move the finger away from your mouth to show that we are safer when we can talk about our problems.

Keep telling until you get help

Pretend that your hands are talking to each other. One hand asks, "I need help." The other hand replies, "I will help you."

Safety Signals for the Kidpower Safety Rule that "Touch, play, or games for fun or affection should be safe, the choice of each person, allowed by the adults in charge, and not a secret, which means that others can know."

Safe

Hug yourself to show that we all deserve to be and feel safe.

The choice of each person

Put two thumbs up to show that each person needs to agree about touch or games for fun or affection.

Allowed by the adults in charge

Curl up your fingers and move your hand up and down to show the head of the adult in charge nodding in approval.

Others Can Know

Raise both arms above your head with your palms facing up to show that touch, play, and affection should NOT be a secret.

The full set of Kidpower Safety Signals can be downloaded from our online Library at www.kidpower.org

 A publication of Kidpower Teenpower Fullpower International® www.kidpower.org For permission to copy, contact safety@kidpower.org

Discussions And Practices To Build Understanding And Skills

Fullpower Safety Comics provides important tools for teens and adults wanting to learn how to take charge of their emotional and physical safety with people. In addition, this book is useful for professionals who want to introduce People Safety ideas and skills to others. The more that everyone in a family, school, workplace, organization, or community has a common understanding about safety, the safer we are.

Here is how to make discussing, practicing, and using these skills successful.

1. We will be safer and have better relationships if we keep using these skills in everyday life. Discuss or think about the ideas here and then act out the examples shown in the drawings. You can do this by yourself taking on different roles, with a partner, or with a group. Coach each other to be successful in avoiding and solving problems with people.

2. Don't let discomfort get in the way of safety. Review your Safety Plans and the People Safety skills in this book on a regular basis. Give special attention to actions that might be hard due to embarrassment, such as interrupting busy adults when you have a problem, yelling to get help, or speaking up if someone is bullying. Remember that feeling embarrassed, upset, or shy is normal, but it is important not to let these emotions stop us from getting help or making the safest choices.

3. Be a bridge to others by adapting these examples and ideas for each individual's age, life situation, and abilities. If necessary, simplify by using fewer words or changing the wording to ensure understanding and relevance. You can also expand on the concepts presented by discussing how to adapt these skills and ideas to handle more complicated situations that might not be covered in this book.

4. Instead of testing or tricking people, coach them to be successful. When you are practicing, pause to give people a chance to try to use the skill. If they get stuck, coach them in exactly what to say, how to say it, and what to do with their bodies, as if you were the director or a prompter in a play. Encourage people to project an assertive attitude of both power and respect in their body language, choice of words, and posture, rather than acting either passively or aggressively.

5. Make the practices fun by being upbeat rather than anxious, rewarding small steps with encouragement, and celebrating progress rather than looking for perfection. To be safe, people need to know both what to do and how to do it in a positive, powerful way. With each activity, be sure to remind anyone who might take something you are saying or doing personally that "We are just pretending so that we can practice."

6. Keep the focus on how to stay safe rather than on the bad things that can happen. Going into detail about the ways we can get hurt just makes people anxious without making anyone safer. Worrying and talking about safety problems can feel as if we are doing something—but are not nearly as effective as actually having a clear plan and practicing how to implement it so that we are prepared to take action.

7. Give discussing, practicing, and using these skills the same priority that you give other issues related to health and safety. These are crucial skills that can prevent problems and make daily life safer and more fun. If you encounter resistance, acknowledge that it is normal to not want to practice and to feel as if we already know what do. However, rehearsing how to handle different kinds of problems is for our safety and must be a high priority. Discussing is not the same as actually practicing. Even if they express lots of resistance, most people also enjoy showing you and themselves that they know what to do.

Make the Kidpower Put Safety First Commitment for Yourself and Others (page 6)

Make this commitment to help you remember to Put Safety First: "I WILL put the safety and well-being of myself and others ahead of anyone's embarrassment, inconvenience, or offense—including my own!" Think about how this applies to real-life situations such as the ones shown in this book.

Directions for discussion and practices

At any age, we can all be students and teachers for each other—and you can even be your own teacher and your own student! The explanations below are for the person who is leading the discussion or practice. The students are the ones who are participating in these activities with the support of the leader.

Put Safety First (pages 7 to 8)

Our Underlying Principle is that the safety and self-esteem of each person are more important than anyone's embarrassment, inconvenience, or offense. The problem is that these feelings are powerful and uncomfortable, so they can get in the way of wise choices. Use the examples for ideas on discussing or thinking about how safety comes first.

Showing awareness, calm, and respectful confidence (page 9)

People will usually bother you less and listen to you more if you act aware, calm, respectful, and confident. Close your body down like the drawings show and then notice the difference when you stand or sit tall and turn your head to look around. Stand behind someone and do something silly for this person to notice and report to you what they saw, so they can practice their awareness.

Act more safe, not less safe (page 10)

Feeling worried or scared when someone is acting threatening, or getting angry if someone is calling you names is normal. However, it is safer to stay calm and respectful on the outside, to leave, and to go and get help. Remind yourself and others that we can all decide to make safe choices in how we ACT, no matter how we FEEL inside. To practice, act out the situations shown in order to feel and see the difference between acting oblivious, scared, and/or angry—or aware, calm, respectful, and confident.

Practice Getting Centered by taking a breath, straightening your back, feeling where your hands and feet are, and focusing on something positive near you. Practice sounding and looking powerful, clear, and respectful.

Use different types of power (pages 11 to 13)

There are many ways to be powerful that do not involve fighting. We have found doing something physical helps people to remember some of the different ways to be powerful.

Squeeze your lips together to use Mouth Closed Power instead of saying something you shouldn't. Raise your hand as if to hit someone or to touch something you shouldn't and pull your hands down to your side to use your Hands Down Power. Touch your ears to remember Listening Power. Walk your fingers like little legs along your arm to remember to use Walk Away Power. If someone uses a wheelchair, roll your fingers along your arm to remember Roll Away Power.

Coach anyone you are practicing with to follow your lead. Discuss who actually starts the fight in the Mei Lin Uses Her Walk Away Power Story. Discuss how Mei Lin uses different powers in the Mei Lin Protects Herself From Being Pushed Story.

Pay attention to who is around and know your Safety Plan (pages 14 to 17)

Develop assessment skills by asking yourself and others questions. Make a list of every place you go. What sorts of safety problems might come up? Do you know how to get help if you need it?

Things to think about include: whether the place is isolated or has many people or places to go to for help; whether you are going to be on your own or with a friend or family member; and how you can persist in getting help if someone doesn't help you at first. Being able to be persistent and overcoming embarrassment is an important part of being safe out in the world. To practice, act out solving a safety problem on the bus or going home from school or work.

Checking and Thinking First before you change your plan (page 18)

We are all safer when the people who care about us know where we are, who is with us, and what we are doing, including with people we know. And we are safer if we assess safety before we let someone we don't know well get close to us, especially in an isolated place and if we notice right away when things change in the place or in the person's behavior that might make a situation less safe.

Practice in your mind or with others how to Think First and let others know BEFORE you change your plan using relevant examples, such as: before you open the door; before you go with a friendly neighbor even if this is someone you know who invites you to do something fun; before you go with someone you don't know well who says that an authority figure such as a parent told you to go with them; and before you get close to someone you don't know well who is asking for directions, trying to talk with you, or trying to give you something.

Pretend to be someone approaching the students in a friendly way and coach them one at a time to stand up, move away, and go to Check First with their adults; to Think First and let housemates know; or to call or text their adults to get permission before they change their plans. Now pretend that they are waiting for a ride and that you are someone they know but didn't expect coming to pick them up. Say, "Your ____ (mom, dad, adult friend) says to come with me." Coach students to move away and go to where they can call, saying, "I need to Check First for myself."

Think First before you open your door to someone you were not expecting (page 19)

Remember that being safe is more important than being polite. You can choose whether and when to answer the door, answer an e-mail message, or talk to someone on the phone. Use the examples to practice how NOT to answer the door.

Stranger Safety (page 20)

Most people are good, but a few people do bad things. The truth is most people who bother us are actually people we know, but it is important to remember that even though we can feel close to someone we don't know quite quickly, it takes a while for our relationship with someone to grow from being a stranger, to an acquaintance, to a friend. Discuss or think about when someone stops being a stranger anymore and how we all need to Think First before we do anything with people we don't know well.

Although most of us know that a stranger is just someone we don't know well, we often have images in our minds about what a stranger we are worried about might look like or how a stranger who will cause trouble might act at first. What do those pictures look like for you?

When we are out in the world, we are often in situations where we can and should be able to talk to a stranger while we are on our own. Our job is to Think First before we take anything from, get close to, or talk to someone we don't know. What is important is that we stay very aware and assess the safety of the situation by noticing if there are a lot of people nearby to help us if we have a problem; by noticing whether someone is approaching lots of people or singling them out; and by not giving out any personal information.

If you are practicing with students, ask them to give you examples of personal information. Practice pretending you are a stranger out in public. Start out just saying hi or asking for the time. Next, ask a question that is personal information (e.g. "Do you live around here? Do you go to ___ school?"). Let students practice changing the subject or moving away if they feel worried or uncomfortable.

You can also practice by approaching students one at a time while calling their name or holding something that belongs to them. People of all ages can be confused when a stranger says their name, because they think they may know the person. We are safest if we Think First even if someone knows our name.

You are more important than your stuff (page 21)

Too many people have gotten hurt because they fought over their stuff.

Pretend to be a friend who wants to borrow money. Coach the person practicing to hold onto the purse or wallet and say firmly but politely, "Sorry, but it doesn't work for me to give you any money."

If someone has limited speaking skills, coach the person to just say, or sign, "No." Pretend to beg and try to make the person feel bad for saying no. Coach the person to persist in setting the boundary by saying, "Sorry, I need my money."

Next, pretend to be someone who is a stranger asking for spare change. Coach the person practicing to leave quickly, saying nothing or, "Sorry, no."

Finally, pretend to be someone dangerous who is robbing them. Coach the person who is practicing to hand over their money and say politely, "Take it. It's yours." and then move away as soon as possible to safety and get help.

Know your Safety Plan if you are having an emergency (pages 15 to 22)
Remember that our safety rules are different in emergencies. We need to know what to do if we are hurt or in trouble, and we cannot immediately get help from people we know.

Getting help from people we don't know well or at all can feel very uncomfortable. To practice, pretend to be a busy, impatient cashier. Coach the people practicing to act out coming to the front of the line, interrupting you, and being persistent in asking for help because they are being bothered by someone, their friend is hurt, or they are lost.

Be persistent in getting help (page 23)
Our goal is to know how to get help everywhere we go. Ask yourself, "Where is Safety?" Discuss where Safety might be in different places. If using a mobile phone is part of the Safety Plan, have a backup plan that involves talking to a person—such as asking a clerk for help, calling police, asking a woman with children, etc. Unless we are having a big emergency, we should not leave the place where the people with us were planning for us to be.

Think about when to wait and when to interrupt. You might need to wait if you want something—but your Safety Plan is to interrupt even busy, impatient adults and be persistent in if you need help.

To practice with students, coach them to imagine that they are lost or being bothered, and to be strong, respectful, and persistent in getting help. Pretend to be a busy, impatient, and rude storekeeper talking to a customer. Coach students to interrupt you firmly and politely by saying, "Excuse me. I have a safety problem." Say, "I'm busy. Go away." Coach them to persist: "I see you are busy but I need help!"

Yell, leave, and get help if you are scared (page 24 to 25)
Yelling in public can feel very embarrassing for people of any age. Put your hands up to make a wall like the characters are doing. Yell words like, "STOP! LEAVE! HELP!" Make a deep short yell from your belly, rather than from your throat.

Think about yelling as loudly as you would want your loved ones to yell if they were in trouble. Practice yelling together to help everyone build strength and confidence in their voices.

If practicing with students, pretend to be someone acting unsafe by pointing at students one at a time and yelling "Blah! Blah! Blah!" Coach them to put their hands in front of their bodies like a wall and to yell, "STOP!" As the pretend attacker, act startled, and stop. Giving a response is very important to help students build their belief in the power of yelling.

Coach them to run or walk quickly (or roll in a wheelchair) to Safety yelling, "I NEED HELP!" Have someone act as the Safety person they go to, and coach this person to say, "I will help you."

Arm Grab Escape (page 25)
Practice the arm grab escape with students one at a time by grabbing one of their arms gently but firmly. When practicing, you are holding your students' arms hard enough so they feel a little trapped, but not so hard that you bruise them, injure them, or make it impossible for them to escape. The goal is for them to learn the technique.

Have a student stand up in front of you and grab their arm making sure there is enough room around you so you do not bump into things when practicing. Keep in mind that students will be pulling away from you so they need more space behind them. Coach them to clasp their hands together (make sure they are not intertwining their fingers) and use the leverage of their arm by turning and moving their body away and keeping their arm close to their body. When practicing, they should loudly shout "NO" when they pull away—and then also practice going to safety.

The first time you practice, let go as soon as you feel a student pull against you. Students can pull away with a lot of force, so be prepared and make sure they are also in balance and prepared to catch themselves when they pull away. Then let the student practice again and hold on a little tighter. Coach students to pull their hands out against the place where your fingertips come together with your thumb, because this spot is the weakest part of someone's grip. Coach them to loudly yell "NO!" and "HELP!" while pulling away.

Know how to set and respect boundaries with people you know (pages 26 to 27)
Discuss the boundary introduction and how theses ideas work in real life.

To practice, pretend to be a friend who bothers others by poking them as a joke. Don't actually poke—just act like you are going to. Coach the people practicing to make their body tall, look at you, and say, "Please stop" using an assertive voice and body language. Respond by saying, "Okay!"

Next, do the "May I have a hug?" practice. Coach the other person to ask you, "May I have a hug?" Say, "No thanks. No hugs today. We can wave." Both of you smile and wave. Reverse roles so you are the one to ask, "May I have a hug?" Coach the other person to say, "No thanks. No hugs today. Just wave." Both of you smile and wave.

Protect yourself from being hurt by name-calling (pages 28 to 33)
Think about different kinds of words that hurt that others say to you or that you say to yourself. Act out using the different kinds of trash cans and affirmations shown in the drawings. For example, put a hand on your hip and show that the hole makes a personal Trash Can.

Practice together using language that is relevant for each person. For example, suppose that someone says, "You're stupid." You can catch the word "stupid" and throw it into your personal Trash Can, and then put your hand on your heart and say, "I am smart!"

If you are practicing with students, YOU are the one who is giving the insult for students to practice throwing away—being sure that they are prepared to do this successfully—and have some positive self-talk ready to take care of their feelings. Don't let students be the ones who are giving the insults unless they can do this in a way that is emotionally safe.

Discuss other positive ways to dispose of hurtful messages. Practice with words or attitudes that might be bothering each person. The goal is to protect your own feelings while not being insulting to the person who was acting unkind, as this could cause a confrontation.

Now, practice giving each other compliments while the other person takes them in. In daily life, try to give each other genuine compliments as often as you can. At all ages, people are often very hard on themselves and feel a lot of pressure to look and act a certain way. They need to hear over and over d how much people love and care about them just the way they are.

Stop unwanted touch (pages 34 to 36)
Healthy boundaries about affection include people being able to ask for what they want, accepting a no answer, realizing when they don't want some kinds of touch or attention, and being able to say so. Most people don't like being told what to do or not do. We need to know how to persist in protecting our boundaries in case someone doesn't notice, doesn't listen, tries to make us feel wrong by using emotional coercion, offers a bribe, or makes us promise not to tell. We need to be prepared to use our voices, bodies, and words to set strong and respectful boundaries with people we know, such as family, friends, and peers.

To practice with students, ask for a hug and coach students to say, "No, thanks! Let's just wave!" Coach students to ask you for a hug so you can say, "No, thanks! Let's just shake hands."

In these practices, YOU take on the role of the person who is causing the problem, making sure that you are coaching students to be successful. Unless they can do this in a way that is emotionally safe, do not have students act out pretending to be the one who is pushing against someone's boundaries.

Pretend to bother students one at a time by touching them on their shoulders. Ask, "Do you like this? If you like this touch, it is fine. But can you change your mind? Yes, you can. Now, pretend you don't like this touch any more." Coach students to give you back your hand in a firm, polite way and say, in a clear, respectful voice, "Please stop." Pretend not to listen, and put your hand back. Coach students to stand up and move back, make a fence with their hands, look at you, and say in a powerful and respectful way, "I said, 'Please stop!' I don't like it."

Next, pretend to be sad or annoyed so students can practice dealing with emotional coercion. Say, "But I like you. I thought you were my friend." Coach students to project an assertive attitude while they say, "I don't mean to hurt your feelings and I am your friend, and I still want you to stop." Or just, "Sorry and stop!"

Discuss when bribes are safe or unsafe. Practice resisting unsafe bribes. Say, "I'll give you a_____ (a treat, some money, or something else you think the person you are practicing with would like) if you let me touch your shoulder after you asked me to stop. But don't tell anybody, okay?" Coach each student to say, "Stop or I'll tell!"

Pretend to get angry or upset without acting intensely or making specific threats. Say, "Promise not to tell anyone or something bad will happen!" Or, "You have to promise not to tell or I won't be able to hang out with you anymore." Or, "Please don't tell, or I could get into trouble." Coach students to say, "I won't tell if you stop." Say, "Most of the time, our values are to tell the truth and keep our promises. But you can lie and break a promise to stay safe, as long as you get away as soon as you can and tell an adult you trust and keep telling until someone does something about it."

Get help from people you trust when you have a problem and keep asking until you get the help you need (pages 37 to 38)

Remember that touch, teasing, activities, videos, photos, presents others give you, and any kind of problem should not have to be secret, which means others can know. Discuss or think about how to find people you can count on to help you if you have a problem. Remember that it is NOT your fault if you have a safety problem even if you made a mistake or feel embarrassed, and it is NEVER too late to tell, so keep telling until you get help.

To practice with students, tell them one at a time to pretend to have a safety problem. You pretend to be a busy adult (act as if you are reading a book, texting, or working). Coach students to interrupt you to ask for help. Say, "I'm busy." Coach them to ask again. Say, "Don't bother me."

Coach them to persist by saying, "This is about my safety." Listen and coach them to tell the whole story. Say, "Thank you for telling me." If students do this well, do the practice again but be unsupportive by saying, "That's your problem. Solve it yourself." Coach them to persist and say, "I tried solving it myself but I don't feel safe. I need help." Or act grumpy and say, "That's your problem." Discuss whom else to tell.

Know what bullying is and how to stop it (pages 39 to 43)

Discuss or think about examples of bullying, teasing, and harassment as they happen in real life, in stories, in games, or in movies, such as shunning, name-calling, intimidation, etc.

To practice with students, pretend to act like someone who is bullying by saying something mean. Coach the person practicing to say, "Stop. That's a hurtful thing to say (or do)!" Next, say, "I can say anything I want." Coach students to use their Imagination Trash Cans to protect their feelings, move away, and get help. Pretend to be someone who is bullying physically. One at a time, push students gently and say something like, "Get over here, you dummy!" Coach them to take a breath, throw the mean word away, use Mouth Closed Power by not answering back, and use Walk Away Power by standing tall, staying calm, and walking with awareness. Remind students to go to someone in charge and get help because problems should not be secrets.

Lead a practice about inclusion. First, practice persisting in being included. Pretend to be playing a game and or having a discussion. Coach students one at a time to walk up to you and say in a cheerful assertive way, "Excuse me. I'd like to join you."

Act out being rejecting by frowning and saying, "Go away. We don't want you here." "Or, You're not good enough." Or, "There are too many playing already."

Coach students to practice persisting by using a calm, clear tone of voice, instead of getting upset. For example, "I'd really like to join you." Or, "I'll get better if I practice." Or, "There's always room for one more." Or, "Give me a chance." Or, "The rule here is everybody gets to participate."

Now, practice leaving. Pretend to be leaving students out and coach them to leave with confidence, approach someone else who seems to be alone, and reach out in a friendly and confident way by asking, "Do you mind if I join you?" Have that person respond by saying cheerfully, "Sure!"

Now, practice advocacy skills. Pretend to be unkind to someone else. Coach students to say, "Stop. That is not kind!" Or, "That's a hurtful thing to say. Please stop!" Or, "Let her join us!"

Being safe with technology (pages 44 to 45)
Online technology is great because is helps us share information and connect with people far away. Discuss or think about the different ways that technology helps people, and come up with safe and unsafe ways you can use technology. Discuss or think about how you can keep yourself safe while using computers and cell phones.

Be safe with your friends (pages 46 to 48)
Discuss or think about the different examples of when people are being safe or unsafe and how to use the peer pressure tactics. Using specific situations from real life, rehearse words and actions that can help solve different safety problems with friends.

Using Personal Safety Skills to Develop Better Relationships (pages 49 to 66)
There are lots of problems that People Safety skill can help to avoid, prevent, or solve. Dating, friends being thoughtless or unkind, people being prejudiced, being unkind to ourselves, problems in our families, or witnessing violence are all problems that can leave us feeling unsafe, uncomfortable, angry, or sad.

To practice, pick stories about situations in your own life or the lives of people you care about. Act out the strategies and skills that the characters are using to solve these problems. If there is an issue you'd like us to cover, let us know!

Finally, Discuss the Kidpower Protection Promise for All Ages and Abilities (Page 67) with everyone important to you!

Kidpower Services For All Ages And Abilities

Overview

Kidpower Teenpower Fullpower International is a global nonprofit leader dedicated to providing effective and empowering child protection, positive communication, and personal safety skills for all ages and abilities. Since 1989, Kidpower has served over 3 million children, teenagers, and adults, including those with difficult life challenges, locally and around the world through our in-person workshops, educational resources, and partnerships. We give our students the opportunity for successful practice of "People Safety" skills in ways that helps prepare them to develop healthy relationships, increase their confidence, take charge of their emotional and physical safety, and act safely and respectfully towards others. For more information, visit www.kidpower.org or contact safety@kidpower.org.

Workshops

Through our centers and traveling instructors, Kidpower has led workshops in over 60 countries spanning six continents. Our programs include: Parent/Caregiver seminars; Parent-Child workshops; training for educators and other professionals; classroom workshops; Family workshops; Teenpower self-defense workshops for teens; Collegepower for young people leaving home; Fullpower self-defense and boundary-setting workshops for adults; Seniorpower for older people; adapted programs for people with special needs; and workplace safety, communication, and team-building seminars. Our three-day Child Protection Advocates Training Institute prepares educators and other professionals, as well as parents and other caring adults, to use Kidpower's intervention, advocacy, and personal safety skills in their personal and professional lives.

Online Library

Our extensive online Library provides over 100 free People Safety resources including articles, videos, webinars, blogs, and podcasts. Free downloads of online publications like our Kidpower Safety Signals, coloring book, and handouts are available for individual use. We provide licensing for use of materials or content for charitable and educational purposes.

Books

We publish an extensive preschool through high school curriculum, as well as books about personal safety for adults, including: *The Kidpower Book for Caring Adults: Personal Safety, Self-Protection, Confidence, and Advocacy for Young People*; cartoon-illustrated *Safety Comics* and *Teaching Books* for children, teens, and adults; *Bullying: What Adults Need to Know and Do to Keep Kids Safe*; *Fullpower Relationship Safety Skills Handbook for Teens and Adults*; *One Strong Move: Cartoon-Illustrated Self-Defense Lessons*; *Earliest Teachable Moment: Personal Safety for Babies, Toddlers, and Preschoolers*; and *Face Bullying with Confidence: Creating Cultures of Respect and Safety for All Ages and Stages of Life*. Please visit our website bookstore for a complete list.

Coaching, Consulting, and Curriculum Development

Long-distance coaching by video-conferencing, telephone, and e-mail enables us to make our services accessible worldwide. We consult with a wide range of experts, organizations, and schools on how best to adapt our program to meet unserved needs and develop new curriculum to increase the People Safety knowledge for different people facing difficult life challenges.

Instructor Training and Center Development

Our very comprehensive certified instructor training program prepares qualified people to teach our programs and to establish centers and offices for organizing services in their communities under our organizational umbrella.

Acknowledgments

Kidpower is a tapestry of many different threads woven by many different hands. Our curriculum has grown from the ideas, questions, teaching, feedback, and stories of countless people since I first started working on child protection, personal safety, and self-defense issues in 1985.

I want to express my appreciation to each of our Kidpower instructors, board members, honorary trustees, senior program leaders, center directors, workshop organizers, advisors, volunteers, donors, parents, students, funding partners, service partners, family members, advocates, hosts, and office staff.

Thank you for the thought, care, time, and generosity that you have given to bring Kidpower Teenpower Fullpower International to where we are today. I feel honored to have you as colleagues and as friends.

Writing each person's story would be a book unto itself. You can learn about the remarkable people who have built and keep building our organization by reading *A Tapestry Woven By Many Different Hands* on our website.

I want to give special acknowledgment to people who have helped to create our cartoon-illustrated Safety Comics and Teaching Books series in many different ways.

Amanda Golert is a Senior Program Leader, Training and Curriculum Consultant, and our Sweden Center Director since 1999. Amanda's role has been crucial in the development of all of our cartoon-illustrated books as the artist, designer, and primary editor.

Timothy Dunphy, our Program Co-Founder, worked with me for many years to create our curriculum and still teaches and serves as a member of our training team.

Senior Program Leader **Chantal Keeney** provided major help with editing, teaching instructions, and content development of our original cartoon-illustrated curriculum.

Our California Program Director **Erika Leonard**; Montreal Center Director **Marylaine Léger**; New Zealand Center Co-Director **Cornelia Baumgartner**; Colorado Center Director **Jan Isaacs Henry**; and Chicago Center Director **Joe Connelly**, who also are all Senior Program Leaders, have each contributed important ideas and improvements to these Kidpower social stories, explanations, and skills over the years.

Finally, thank you to Kidpower Instructor and Senior Program Leader **John Luna-Sparks**, LCSW, CMP, for many years of support, including working with me to create our original Safety Signals.

About The Author

Irene van der Zande is the Founder and Executive Director of Kidpower Teenpower Fullpower International, a global non-profit leader dedicated to protecting people of all ages and abilities from bullying, violence, and abuse by empowering them with knowledge and skills.

Since 1989, Kidpower has served over 3 million children, teenagers, and adults, including those with special needs, through its positive and practical workshops, extensive free online Library, and publications.

Since Kidpower began, Irene has led the development of programs, training of instructors, and establishment of centers, working with a wide range of international experts in education, public safety, violence prevention, mental health, and the martial arts.

Irene has authored numerous books and articles in the child development, child protection, positive communication, and violence and abuse prevention and intervention fields, including the following:

The Parent/Toddler Group: A Model of Effective Intervention to Facilitate Normal Growth and Development, which is published by Cedars-Sinai Medical Center and used as a textbook for mental health and child education professionals; *1, 2, 3... The Toddler Years: A Guide for Parents and Caregivers*, which is used as a textbook in early childhood development programs in many colleges and has a foreword by early childhood development and Respect for Infant Educarers founder Magda Gerber; T*he Kidpower Book for Caring Adults*, a comprehensive guide on personal safety, self-protection, confidence, and advocacy for young people; *Bullying: What Adults Need to Know and Do To Keep Kids Safe*, which is used in the anti-bullying programs of many families, schools, and youth organizations; and the cartoon-illustrated *Kidpower Safety Comics Series* and *Preschool to Young Adult Curriculum Teaching Books*, which provide entertaining and effective tools for introducing and practicing safety skills with young people.

About The Illustrator

Amanda Golert is an experienced self-defense instructor, trainer, passionate advocate for personal safety for children and other vulnerable people, the Center Director of Kidpower Sweden—and she also likes to draw!

For over 15 years, Amanda has supported the growth and development of Kidpower Teenpower Fullpower International. She works in partnership with Irene to illustrate, edit, and design the Kidpower cartoon books and many other educational materials.

 A publication of Kidpower Teenpower Fullpower International® www.kidpower.org For permission to copy, contact safety@kidpower.org

CPSIA information can be obtained
at www.ICGtesting.com
Printed in the USA
LVOW06s0156090916

503872LV00002BD/3/P

9 780971 517820